100

Jokes for Kids

Uncle Amon

Copyright © 2016 Uncle Amon

All rights reserved.

ISBN-13: 978-1536846324
ISBN-10: 1536846325

"A good laugh is sunshine in the house."

— William Thackeray

CONTENTS

WHAT IS A JOKE? i

ANIMAL JOKES 1

MONSTER JOKES 10

SCHOOL JOKES 13

SPORTS JOKES 15

KNOCK KNOCK JOKES 18

HALLOWEEN JOKES 22

THANKSGIVING JOKES 24

CHRISTMAS JOKES 26

ABOUT THE AUTHOR 29

WHAT IS A JOKE?

joke - something said or done to provoke laughter or cause amusement, as a witticism, a short and amusing anecdote, or a prankish act.

Did you know?

Laughter can have positive physical and mental effects on your body. Laughter can make you feel happy and help create bonds with friends and family.

Jokes come in many forms. It can be a one-liner, question and answer, silly stories, funny movies, and lots more.

Share a laugh with a friend today!

ANIMAL JOKES

Q: What do you get when a chicken lays an egg on top of a barn?

A: An eggroll!

Q: What does a bee get at McDonalds?

A: A humburger!

Q: What do cats like to eat on a hot day?

A: A bowl of mice cream!

Q: What is worse than a dog howling at the moon?

A: Two dogs howling at the moon!

Q: What happens when the cows refuse to be milked?

A: Udder chaos!

Q: What dinosaur loves pancakes?

A: A tri-syrup-tops!

Q: How do you tell the difference between an elephant and a mouse?

A: Try picking them up!

Q: Why are fish so gullible?

A: They always fall for the hook, line, and sinker!

Q: How does a mouse stop a video?

A: Hits the paws button!

Q: What do you get when a rabbit gets a perm?

A: Curly hare!

Q: What happened when the owl lost her voice?

A: She did not give a hoot!

Q: What are the smartest bees?

A: Spelling bees!

Q: Which game did the cat want to play with the mouse?

A: Catch!

Q: What do you call a happy Lassie?

A: Jolly collie!

Q: What did one dairy cow say to another?

A: Got milk?

Q: What dinosaur would you find in a rodeo?

A: Bronco-saurus!

Q: What do you call an elephant that cannot read?

A: Dumbo!

Q: How do fish run a business?

A: The start on a small scale!

Q: How did the mouse make gold soup?

A: She put in 14 carrots!

Q: How can you tell which rabbits are the oldest?

A: Look for gray hares.

Q: What kind of birds do you usually find locked up?

A: Jail birds!

Q: How do fireflies start a race?

A: Ready, steady, and glow!

Q: How is cat food sold?

A: Purr can!

Q: What kind of dog is a human's best friend?

A: Palmatian!

Q: How does a cow do math?

A: With a cowculator!

Q: What was the most flexible dinosaur?

A: Tyrannosaurus Flex!

Q: Why did the elephant eat the candle?

A: He wanted a light snack!

Q: Why didn't Noah fish much while on the arc?

A: He only had two worms!

Q: How do mice celebrate a new home?

A: Mouse warming party!

Q: What do you call a rooster who wakes you up at the same time every morning?

A: Alarm cluck!

Q: Where do you take a sick wasp?

A: To the waspital!

Q: Why did the turkey cross the road?

A: To prove he was not a chicken!

Q: What's the unluckiest kind of cat to have?

A: A catastrophe!

Q: Why is it called a litter of puppies?

A: They mess up the whole house!

Q: What is as big as an elephant but weighs nothing?

A: The elephant's shadow!

Q: If you mixed a cow with a flock of ducks, what would you get?

A: Milk and quackers!

Q: What's the scariest dinosaur?

A: A terror-dactyl!

Q: Why do elephants live in the jungle?

A: They do not have to pay rent there!

Q: Where do fish go to borrow money?

A: A loan shark!

Q: What does a 100 pound mouse say to a cat?

A: Here kitty, kitty!

Q: What do you call a chocolate Easter bunny in the sun?

A: A runny bunny!

MONSTER JOKES

Q: What does the hungry monster get after he's eaten too much ice cream?

A: More ice cream!

Q: What monster plays the most April Fools jokes?

A: Prankenstein!

Q: What do you call a huge, ugly, slobbering, furry monster with earplugs in his ears?

A: Anything you like. He can't hear you!

Q: What do sea monsters have for dinner?

A: Fish and ships!

Q: On which day do monsters eat people?

A: Chewsday!

Q: What do you get if you cross a monster with a flea?

A: Lots of very worried dogs!

Q: What should you do if a monster runs through your front door?

A: Run through the back door!

Q: What do they have for lunch at Monster School?

A: Human beans, boiled legs, pickled bunions and eyes-cream.

Q: What does a monster mom say to her kids at dinnertime?

A: Don't talk with someone in your mouth!

Q: What kind of monster can sit on the end of your finger?

A: The boogey man (booger)!

SCHOOL JOKES

Q: What's the worst thing you're likely to find in the school cafeteria?

A: The food!

Q: What did you learn in school today?

A: Not enough. I have to go back tomorrow!

Q: Why was the principal worried?

A: There were too many rulers in school!

Q: What ten letter word starts with g-a-s?

A: Automobile!

Q: What did one math book say to the other?

A: Man I got a lot of problems!

Q: How can you spell too much with two letters?

A: XS (excess)

Q: What's black and white all over and difficult?

A: An exam paper!

Q: Why did the teacher wear sunglasses?

A: Because his class was so bright!

SPORTS JOKES

Q: What did the coach scream to the snack machine?

A: Give me my quarterback!

Q: How do you stop squirrels from playing football in the garden?

A: Hide the ball. It will drive them nuts!

Q: What lights up a tennis court?

A: A tennis match!

Q: What does a basketball player do before he blows out his candles?

A: He makes a swish!

Q: Why did the golfers leave?

A: They heard Tiger was on the course.

Q: Why was Cinderella cut from the team?

A: She ran away from the ball!

Q: Why do marathon runners make good students?

A: Because an education pays off in the long run!

Q: Why did the soccer ball quit?

A: It was tired of getting kicked around!

Q: How come dogs do not like the long baseball schedule?

A: It is ruff playing that many games!

Q: What is a runner's favorite subject in school?

A: Jog-raphy!

KNOCK KNOCK JOKES

Knock knock!

Who's there?

Summer!

Summer who?

Summer good and summer bad!

Knock knock!

Who's there?

Aileen!

Aileen who?

Aileen against the door!

Knock knock!

Who's there?

Moo!

Moo who?

Are you a cow or an owl?

Knock knock!

Who's there?

Becca!

Becca who?

Becca the net!

Knock knock!

Who's there?

Vanna!

Vanna who?

Vanna go to the movies?

Knock knock!

Who's there?

Beets!

Beets who?

Beets me. I forgot the joke!

Knock knock!

Who's there?

Canoe!

Canoe who?

Canoe come out and play?

Knock knock!

Who's there?

Ben!

Ben who?

Ben knocking on this door all day long!

Knock knock!

Who's there?

Nadia!

Nadia who?

Nadia head if you are paying attention!

Knock knock!

Who's there?

Etch!

Etch who?

Bless You!

Knock knock!

Who's there?

Auntie!

Auntie who?

Auntie glad to see me!

HALLOWEEN JOKES

Q: Why was the student witch so bad at essays?

A: Because she could not spell properly!

Q: What do ghosts drink in the morning?

A: Coffee with two screams and one sugar!

Q: How do warty witches keep their hair in place?

A: With scare spray!

Q: What did the little ghost eat for lunch?

A: A booloney sandwich!

Q: Where do baby ghosts go during the day?

A: Day-scare centers!

Q: What do you call two witches who share a room?

A: Broom-mates!

Q: Which day of the week do ghosts like best?

A: Moandays!

THANKSGIVING JOKES

Q: What's the best thing to put into an apple pie?

A: Your teeth!

Q: Why did the Pilgrims want to come to America in the spring?

A: It was rumored that April showers bring Mayflowers!

Q: Why was the Thanksgiving soup worth so much?

A: It was made from 24 carrots!

Q: What did the monster say to the Thanksgiving turkey?

A: Pleased to eat you!

Q: Who is never hungry at Thanksgiving?

A: The turkey because he is always stuffed!

Q: What did the turkey say to the turkey hunter?

A: Quack! Quack!

CHRISTMAS JOKES

Q: Which of Santa's reindeers needs to mind his manners the most?

A: Rude-olph!

Q: Is it true that mummies love Christmas?

A: Yes! Because of all the wrapping!

Q: What is the snowman's favorite snack?

A: Ice crispies!

Q: Why is it so cold at Christmas?

A: Because it's in Decembrrr!

Q: How do sheep in Mexico say Merry Christmas?

A: Fleece Navidad!

Q: What do snowmen do on the weekend?

A: Chill out!

Q: What songs do Santa's gnomes sing to him when he comes home freezing on Christmas night?

A: Freeze a jolly good fellow!

ABOUT THE AUTHOR

Uncle Amon began his career with a vision. It was to influence and create a positive change in the world through children's books by sharing fun and inspiring stories.

Whether it is an important lesson or just creating laughs, Uncle Amon provides insightful stories that are sure to bring a smile to your face! His unique style and creativity stand out from other children's book authors, because he uses real life experiences to tell a tale of imagination and adventure.

"I always shoot for the moon. And if I miss? I'll land in the stars."
-Uncle Amon

Copyright © 2016 Uncle Amon Books. All rights reserved. No part of this book or this book as a whole may be used, reproduced, or transmitted in any form or means without written permission from the publisher. Graphics and images used in this book are licensed and © Dollar Photo Club.

30

Made in the USA
Middletown, DE
09 October 2016